Collins

11+
Verbal
Reasoning

Practice Papers
Book 3

Shelley Welsh

Introduction

The 11+ tests

In most cases, the 11+ selection tests are set by GL Assessment, CEM or the individual school. You should be able to find out which tests your child will be taking on the website of the school they are applying to or from the local authority.

These single subject practice test papers are designed to reflect the style of GL Assessment tests, but provide useful practice and preparation for all 11+ tests and common entrance exams.

The score achieved on these test papers is no guarantee that your child will achieve a score of the same standard on the formal tests. Other factors, such as the standard of responses from all pupils who took the test, will determine their success in the formal examination.

Collins also publishes practice test papers, in partnership with The 11 Plus Tutoring Academy, to support preparation for the CEM tests.

Contents

This book contains:

- four practice papers – Tests A, B, C and D
- a multiple-choice answer sheet for each test
- a complete set of answers, including explanations.

Further multiple-choice answer sheets can be downloaded from our website so that you can reuse these papers: collins.co.uk/11plus

Verbal reasoning

It is particularly important to provide verbal reasoning practice as your child may not have come across these types of question before. Verbal reasoning assesses a child's ability to use, understand and analyse language. The tests assess comprehension and vocabulary. They also include questions that require careful analysis of word structures, patterns and spellings. They require logical thought and reasoning, including the ability to look for patterns and identify relationships between words.

Verbal reasoning tests give schools an insight into a child's ability to interpret, understand, use and manipulate words. These skills are fundamental to learning and so give an indication of a child's potential for learning across the curriculum.

Verbal reasoning measures one aspect of a child's cognitive ability and should not be confused with IQ.

Getting ready for the tests

Spend some time talking with your child before they take the tests, so that they understand the purpose of the practice papers and how doing them will help them to prepare for the actual exam.

Agree with your child a good time to take the practice papers. This should be when they are fresh and alert. You also need to find a good place to work, a place that is comfortable and free from distractions. Being able to see a clock is helpful as they learn how to pace themselves.

Explain how they may find some parts easy and others more challenging, but that they need to have a go at every question. If they 'get stuck' on a question, they should just mark it with an asterisk and carry on. At the end of the paper, they may have time to go back and try again.

Multiple-choice tests

For this style of test, the answers are recorded on a separate answer sheet and not in the book. This answer sheet will often be marked by a computer in the actual exam, so it is important that it is used correctly. Answers should be indicated by drawing a clear pencil line through the appropriate box and there should be no other marks. If your child indicates one answer and then wants to change their response, the first mark must be fully rubbed out. Practising with an answer sheet now will reduce the chance of your child getting anxious or confused during the actual test.

How much time should be given?

Allowing 50 minutes for each of these practice papers will give your child experience of the most likely test format. If your child has not finished after 50 minutes, ask them to draw a line to indicate where they are on the paper at that time, and allow them to finish. This allows them to practise every question type, as well as allowing you to get a score showing how many were correctly answered in the time available. It will also help you and your child to think about ways to increase speed of working if this is an area that your child finds difficult. If your child completes the paper in less than 50 minutes, encourage them to go through and check their answers carefully.

Marking

Award one mark for each correct answer. Half marks are not allowed. No marks are deducted for wrong answers.

If scores are low, look at the paper and identify which question types seem to be harder for your child. Then spend some time going over them together. If your child is very accurate and gets correct answers, but works too slowly, try getting them to do one of the practice papers with time targets going through. If you are helpful and look for ways to help your child, they will grow in confidence and feel well prepared when they take the actual examinations.

And finally...

Let your child know that tests are just one part of school life and that doing their best is what matters. Plan a fun incentive for after the 11+ tests, such as a day out.

Contents

Practice Test A 5

Practice Test B 13

Practice Test C 21

Practice Test D 29

Answers and Explanations 37

Practice Test A Answer Sheet 49

Practice Test B Answer Sheet 51

Practice Test C Answer Sheet 53

Practice Test D Answer Sheet 55

ACKNOWLEDGEMENTS

The author and publisher are grateful to the copyright holders for permission to use quoted materials and images.

Every effort has been made to trace copyright holders and obtain their permission for the use of copyright material. The author and publisher will gladly receive information enabling them to rectify any error or omission in subsequent editions. All facts are correct at time of going to press.

Published by Collins
An imprint of HarperCollins*Publishers* Limited
1 London Bridge Street
London SE1 9GF

HarperCollins*Publishers*
Macken House
39/40 Mayor Street Upper
Dublin 1
D01 C9W8
Ireland

ISBN 9780008761141

First published 2026

10 9 8 7 6 5 4 3 2 1

© HarperCollins*Publishers* Limited 2026

All rights reserved. No part of this publication may be reproduced, stored in a retrieval system, or transmitted, in any form or by any means, electronic, mechanical, photocopying, recording or otherwise, without the prior permission of Collins.

Without limiting the exclusive rights of any author, contributor or the publisher of this publication, any unauthorised use of this publication to train generative artificial intelligence (AI) technologies is expressly prohibited. HarperCollins also exercise their rights under Article 4(3) of the Digital Single Market Directive 2019/790 and expressly reserve this publication from the text and data mining exception.

British Library Cataloguing in Publication Data.

A CIP record of this book is available from the British Library.

Author: Shelley Welsh
Publisher: Clare Souza
Commissioning Editor: Richard Toms
Project Management: Fiona Watson
Cover Design: Sarah Duxbury and Kevin Robbins
Typesetting: Remington (India)
Production: Bethany Brohm
Printed in India by Multivista Global Pvt. Ltd.

This book contains FSC™ certified paper and other controlled sources to ensure responsible forest management.

For more information visit: www.harpercollins.co.uk/green

Verbal Reasoning
Multiple-Choice
Practice Test A

Read these instructions carefully.

1. You must not open or turn over this booklet until you are told to do so.

2. The booklet is a multiple-choice test containing different types of questions.

3. Each question type begins with an explanation, usually followed by an example.

4. Do all rough working on a separate sheet of paper.

5. You should mark your answers in pencil on the answer sheet provided, not on this booklet.

6. You may have to mark more than one answer (you will be told this in the instructions for the question type). Draw a line firmly through the rectangle next to your answer.

7. Rub out any mistakes as well as you can and mark your new answer.

8. Try to do as many questions as you can. If you find that you cannot do a question, do not waste time on it but go on to the next one.

9. If you are stuck on a question, choose the answer that you think is best.

10. You have 50 minutes to complete the test.

In the following questions, take one letter from the word on the left and add it to the word on the right to make two new, proper words. The original order of the letters within each word must not be changed. Mark the letter that moves on the answer sheet.

Example: stand   ten

Answer: t   (the two new words are 'sand' and 'tent')

1. table   lend
2. spoil   sank
3. clap   fail
4. trusty sigh
5. wine   blow
6. moan   range

In the following questions, the letters stand for numbers. Work out the answer to each sum as a letter and then mark it on the answer sheet.

Example: If A = 2, B = 4, C = 5, D = 8, E = 12

what is the answer to this sum written as a letter?

B × C − E = ?

Answer: D

7. If A = 2, B = 3, C = 6, D = 9, E = 20
what is the answer to this sum written as a letter?
B × C ÷ A = ?

8. If A = 3, B = 23, C = 17, D = 6, E = 9
what is the answer to this sum written as a letter?
A + E + C − D = ?

9. If A = 24, B = 15, C = 5, D = 21, E = 9
what is the answer to this sum written as a letter?
C × E − A = ?

10. If A = 36, B = 24, C = 12, D = 7, E = 21
what is the answer to this sum written as a letter?
A ÷ C + E = ?

NOW GO ON TO THE NEXT PAGE

11. If A = 44, B = 20, C = 13, D = 32, E = 11

    what is the answer to this sum written as a letter?

    A ÷ E × C − B = ?

12. If A = 6, B = 9, C = 12, D = 24, E = 36

    what is the answer to this sum written as a letter?

    E ÷ C × A − B = ?

In the following questions, find the two words, one from each set, which will combine to make one new word, spelt correctly. You cannot change the order of the letters, and the word from the left-hand set always comes first. Mark both words on the answer sheet.

> **Example:**   (back, behind, low)   (front, ground, above)
>
> **Answer:**   back   ground   (the new word is 'background')

13. (cup, hope, tab)   (free, let, full)

14. (near, far, out)   (off, in, by)

15. (date, coup, fast)   (led, fruit, mouse)

16. (truck, car, van)   (nation, rage, wheel)

17. (wide, war, scroll)   (down, fare, world)

18. (mess, tell, miss)   (age, tail, time)

In the following sentences, one word written in capital letters has had three consecutive letters removed. These three missing letters make a three-letter word. Work out the three-letter word. Try out each of the options on the answer sheet to see which one works.

> **Example:**   The **STER** scuttled into the corner of the cage.
>
> **Answer:**   **HAM**   (the word in capitals is **HAMSTER**)

19. Ffion **CONCENTRD** on answering the question.

20. There are **SEVL** reasons why I don't like Brussels sprouts.

21. The criminal **ESED** from prison.

22. There was a slight **SPRLING** of snow on the hills.

23. Mum **REED** to the news with complete surprise.

24. Peter **ACCITALLY** knocked over his drink.

NOW GO ON TO THE NEXT PAGE

The alphabet is given here to help you with the following questions.

A B C D E F G H I J K L M N O P Q R S T U V W X Y Z

In each question there is a series of letters following a pattern. Work out the pattern of the sequence and mark the correct pair of letters to continue the sequence on the answer sheet.

> **Example:** EW FX GY HZ ?
> **Answer:** IA

25. JC   LD   NE   PF   RG   ?
26. TJ   QM   NP   KS   HV   ?
27. RM   VI   AD   GX   NQ   ?
28. CH   EF   FE   FE   EF   ?
29. CC   BE   ZD   WF   SE   ?
30. DQ   FN   CP   EM   BO   ?

Read the information below and then use it to find the correct answer to the question. Mark the answer on the answer sheet.

31. Carla likes cars.
    She drives her red sports car to work.
    Carla lives in the countryside.
    She has a white van.

    Which of the following statements **must** be true?

    A Carla is a farmer.
    B Carla only likes red cars.
    C Carla has at least two vehicles.
    D Carla likes the countryside.
    E Carla likes vans and cars.

In the following questions, there are two sets of words. Choose the two words, one from each set, that are most **opposite** in meaning. Mark them both on the answer sheet.

> **Example:** (late, morning, breakfast)   (bed, early, time)
> **Answer:** late   early

32. (fierce, smooth, relaxed)   (stressed, calmly, silky)
33. (reveal, regard, observe)   (find, excavate, conceal)

NOW GO ON TO THE NEXT PAGE

34.	(pencil, blunt, nib)	(pen, sharp, lead)
35.	(loyal, faithless, promise)	(keep, pretence, unreliable)
36.	(slight, transparent, obscure)	(power, clear, helpless)
37.	(royal, wealthy, scant)	(needy, fulfilled, safe)

In the following sentences, a four-letter word is hidden across the end of one word and the start of the next word. Find the pair of words that contain the four-letter word and mark them on the answer sheet.

> **Example:** Richard ate his delicious breakfast hungrily.
>
> **Answer:** Richard ate   (the hidden word is 'date')

38. The teacher delivered a great lesson.

39. That's our aunt's house on the corner.

40. Please come to the picnic tomorrow.

41. Today is hotter than it was yesterday.

42. It was the best operatic performance ever.

43. We went home after the match.

What number continues the pattern in each series? Mark it on the answer sheet.

> **Example:** 3, 6, 9, 12, ?
>
> **Answer:** 15

44.	1,	10,	19,	28,	37,	?	
45.	22,	23,	25,	28,	32,	?	
46.	26,	20,	15,	11,	8,	6,	?
47.	71,	70,	67,	62,	55,	46,	?
48.	48,	12,	24,	8,	12,	4,	?
49.	121,	112,	100,	85,	67,	?	

NOW GO ON TO THE NEXT PAGE

Read the information below and then use it to find the correct answer to the question. Mark the answer on the answer sheet.

50. A group of children are discussing all the pets they own.

    Brogan has a cat and a dog. Ewan has a goldfish. Joe has twice the number of cats as Brogan. Both Joe and Ewan own a hamster. Brogan also has two lizards. Sophie has two rabbits, two goldfish and a gerbil.

    Which of the following statements **must** be true?

    A Sophie has the most pets.
    B Ewan has more pets than Brogan.
    C Sophie has a lizard.
    D Brogan has two dogs.
    E Joe has twice as many hamsters as Ewan.

In the following questions, one letter can be used to end the first word and start the second word to make four new words. The same letter must be used to complete both pairs of words. Mark the letter on the answer sheet.

> Example: LAM (?) ALE   SNO (?) ILL
> Answer: B   (The four new words are LAMB, BALE, SNOB, BILL)

51. SEVE (?) END   BEAVE (?) EACH
52. BLEAC (?) EAVE   SIG (?) OLD
53. WIC (?) IND   SLIC (?) NOT
54. FLOTILL (?) MBLE   YOG (?) VENGE
55. CAME (?) AUNCH   YEL (?) OAN
56. CLOSE (?) HORN   SPEN (?) URRET

The alphabet is given here to help you with the following questions.

A B C D E F G H I J K L M N O P Q R S T U V W X Y Z

Complete the second pair of letters in the same way as the first pair. Mark the correct letter pair on the answer sheet.

> **Example:** EL is to FM as TU is to ?
>
> **Answer:** UV

57. MQ is to LP as ID is to ?
58. JP is to LS as SW is to ?
59. QZ is to MD as RY is to ?
60. BY is to WF as EV is to ?
61. AZ is to FU as BY is to ?
62. BG is to KA as QR is to ?

In each question, there are two pairs of words. Select and mark a new word that goes equally well with both word pairs from the options on the answer sheet.

> **Example:** (firm, rigid) (tricky, difficult)
>
> **Answer:** hard

63. (revolve, turn) (bread, bun)
64. (see, notice) (smudge, stain)
65. (climb, ascend) (degree, size)
66. (kind, compassionate) (sensitive, painful)
67. (harness, bandage) (hurl, toss)
68. (expensive, costly) (beloved, treasured)

NOW GO ON TO THE NEXT PAGE

In the following questions, the three words on the right-hand side go together in the same way as the three words on the left-hand side. Work out the missing word and mark it on the answer sheet.

> **Example:** dark (yarn) nosy : pear (?) pool
>
> **Answer:** leap

69. pour (pod) bid : left (?) pot
70. crab (bar) bird : stab (?) fear
71. spin (dine) lend : stop (?) team
72. flea (flap) plan : snip (?) kill
73. winds (dine) scare : films (?) crank
74. fair (fret) bent : pair (?) told

In the following sets of five words, find the two words that are **different from** the rest. Mark them both on the answer sheet.

> **Example:** duck   goat   cow   swan   robin
>
> **Answer:** goat   cow

75. cooperate   undertake   collaborate   continue   unite
76. Africa   France   Antarctica   Asia   Italy
77. tornado   rain   hurricane   sleet   snow
78. wool   silk   cotton   nylon   plastic
79. goldfish   toad   crow   frog   newt
80. arid   moist   parched   wet   thirsty

END OF TEST

Verbal Reasoning
Multiple-Choice
Practice Test B

Read these instructions carefully.

1. You must not open or turn over this booklet until you are told to do so.
2. The booklet is a multiple-choice test containing different types of questions.
3. Each question type begins with an explanation, usually followed by an example.
4. Do all rough working on a separate sheet of paper.
5. You should mark your answers in pencil on the answer sheet provided, not on this booklet.
6. You may have to mark more than one answer (you will be told this in the instructions for the question type). Draw a line firmly through the rectangle next to your answer.
7. Rub out any mistakes as well as you can and mark your new answer.
8. Try to do as many questions as you can. If you find that you cannot do a question, do not waste time on it but go on to the next one.
9. If you are stuck on a question, choose the answer that you think is best.
10. You have 50 minutes to complete the test.

In the following questions, there are two sets of words. Choose the two words, one from each set, that are **closest** in meaning. Mark them both on the answer sheet.

Example:	(table, cup, knife)	(chair, fork, mug)
Answer:	cup	mug

1. (crime, thief, police) (prison, jail, offence)
2. (skip, stumble, hop) (stagger, stroll, amble)
3. (delicate, hoarse, special) (sturdy, pretty, fragile)
4. (swindle, succumb, abandon) (prevent, ignore, surrender)
5. (review, resignation, aspect) (feature, essay, assertion)
6. (blatant, bitter, corrupt) (blank, obvious, inconspicuous)

In the following sentences, a four-letter word is hidden across the end of one word and the start of the next word. Find the pair of words that contain the four-letter word and mark them on the answer sheet.

Example:	Richard ate his delicious breakfast hungrily.
Answer:	Richard ate (the hidden word is 'date')

7. Paola likes caring for her little brother.
8. Mimi bought more than one book.
9. Theo read to the young boy.
10. My school had the best uniform.
11. The cake is just about ready.
12. Petra sang the final song of the show.

NOW GO ON TO THE NEXT PAGE

In the following questions, take one letter from the word on the left and add it to the word on the right to make two new, proper words. The original order of the letters within each word must not be changed. Mark the letter that moves on the answer sheet.

> **Example:** stand   ten
>
> **Answer:** t   (The two new words are 'sand' and 'tent')

13. blank   band
14. there   sore
15. batch   lip
16. taint   pint
17. jest   and
18. teach   ear

The three numbers in each group are related in the same way. Find the number that correctly completes the last group. Mark the number on the answer sheet.

> **Example:** (7 [3] 21)   (8 [4] 32)   (9 [?] 45)
>
> **Answer:** 5

19. (41 [6] 35)   (39 [7] 32)   (23 [?] 15)
20. (15 [4] 19)   (11 [16] 27)   (23 [?] 45)
21. (11 [6] 1)   (10 [8] 6)   (16 [?] 2)
22. (19 [20] 3)   (29 [32] 5)   (35 [?] 6)
23. (10 [28] 4)   (8 [22] 3)   (9 [?] 4)
24. (40 [30] 4)   (16 [6] 8)   (18 [?] 3)

NOW GO ON TO THE NEXT PAGE

In the following sets of five words, find the two words that are **different** from the rest. Mark them both on the answer sheet.

> Example: duck goat cow swan robin
>
> Answer: goat cow

25. book   newspaper   write   sign   magazine
26. light   table   switch   chair   desk
27. high jump   cricket   rugby   hurdles   football
28. square   circle   cube   triangle   sphere
29. chase   recover   pursue   follow   find
30. smell   eye   taste   see   ear

In the following questions, some of the words are written in code. The first code word in each question is worked out for you. Using the same code, work out the second code word and mark it on the answer sheet. Remember that if you are working out a word created by the code, you will have to reverse the rule.

The alphabet is given here to help you.

A B C D E F G H I J K L M N O P Q R S T U V W X Y Z

> Example: If the code for **MELT** is **LDKS**, what is the code for **THAW**?
>
> Answer: **SGZV**

31. If the code for **SPEAK** is **URGCM**, what is the code for **NOISE**?

32. If the code for **LOG** is **KNF**, what does **AHM** mean?

33. If the code for **BITE** is **CKWI**, what is the code for **MOAN**?

34. If the code for **SINK** is **QKLM**, what does **NNYP** mean?

35. If the code for **BLOW** is **YHJQ**, what is the code for **SAND**?

36. If the code for **BLUE** is **AIPX**, what is the code for **GREY**?

NOW GO ON TO THE NEXT PAGE

Find the number that will complete the sum correctly. Mark it on the answer sheet.

> Example: 5 + 8 = 6 + [?]
>
> Answer: 7

37. 27 + 18 = 62 − [?]
38. 15 − 7 = 72 ÷ [?]
39. 5 × 3 + 12 − 4 = 32 − [?]
40. 18 ÷ 3 × 7 = 9^2 − [?]
41. 49 ÷ 7 × 8 − 5 = 100 − 77 + [?]
42. 12 × 9 ÷ 3 − 17 = 4 × 20 − [?]

Read the information below and then use it to find the correct answer to the question. Mark the number on the answer sheet.

43. Rajiv, Cameron, Abby, George and Lizzie are in charge of the Christmas class party. They each bring the following items:

    Rajiv brings fruit and sandwiches.
    Cameron brings crisps.
    George and Lizzie bring sandwiches and fruit.
    Everyone except Rajiv brings pizza.
    Abby, George and Lizzie bring juice.

    How many children **do not** bring sandwiches?

In the following questions, choose one word from each set to best complete the sentences. Mark both words on the answer sheet, remembering to use one word from each set.

> Example: **Tall** is to (height, length, short) as **narrow** is to (wide, thin, road).
>
> Answer: short wide

44. **Stars** are to (above, sky, night) as **fish** are to (swimming, chips, ocean).
45. **Eat** is to (ate, food, stomach) as **have** is to (was, had, hold).
46. **Triangle** is to (maths, three, equal) as **octagon** is to (eight, six, shape).
47. **Leaf** is to (stalk, root, plant) as **branch** is to (trunk, bush, twig).
48. **Radio** is to (music, listen, news) as **film** is to (watch, applaud, actor).
49. **Astronaut** is to (space, universe, rocket) as **captain** is to (soldier, ship, army).

NOW GO ON TO THE NEXT PAGE

Find the word that completes the third pair of words in the same way as the first two pairs. Mark the word on the answer sheet.

> **Example:** (kite kit)   (pipe pip)   (seat [?])
> **Answer:** sea

50. (stint tin)   (snore nor)   (cared [?])
51. (suspend spend)   (feeling fling)   (sapling [?])
52. (faint fin)   (swear sea)   (beard [?])
53. (floaty toy)   (cheeky key)   (cornea [?])
54. (honest son)   (finest sin)   (tatter [?])
55. (reward draw)   (hotbed debt)   (peanut [?])

What number continues the pattern in each series? Mark it on the answer sheet.

> **Example:** 3,   6,   9,   12,   ?
> **Answer:** 15

56. 2,   3,   5,   8,   13,   ?
57. 80,   63,   47,   32,   18,   ?
58. −124,   −47,   30,   107,   184,   ?
59. 2^2,   3, 3^2,   8, 4^2,   ?
60. 21,   24,   21,   30,   22,   36,   22,   ?
61. 120,   112,   104,   96,   ?

NOW GO ON TO THE NEXT PAGE

In the following questions, find the two words, one from each set, which will combine to make one new word, spelt correctly. You cannot change the order of the letters and the word from the left-hand set always comes first. Mark both words on the answer sheet.

> **Example:** (back, behind, low) (front, ground, above)
>
> **Answer:** back ground (the new word is 'background')

62. (ant, fly, spider) (web, eat, hem)
63. (cup, see, water) (full, saucer, side)
64. (scar, nail, wound) (cut, let, out)
65. (bike, pump, tyre) (bell, kin, chain)
66. (sing, god, hymn) (send, pray, church)
67. (impress, alter, count) (active, native, change)

In the following sentences, one word written in capital letters has had three letters removed. These three missing letters make a three-letter word. Work out the three-letter word. Try out each of the options on the answer sheet to see which one works.

> **Example:** The **STER** scuttled into the corner of the cage.
>
> **Answer:** HAM (The word in capitals is **HAMSTER**.)

68. I gave Gabbi my book on **DITION** she'd return it the next day.
69. "Can you **DESCE** how you feel?" asked the doctor.
70. In History, we used the computers to **RERCH** the Tudors.
71. My little brother was **PREDING** to be a ghost.
72. Olga **TSLATED** the text into her own language.
73. Mum hung the **WING** on the line.

NOW GO ON TO THE NEXT PAGE

Read the information below and then use it to find the correct answer to the question. Mark the letter on the answer sheet.

74. Five monkeys born on the same day are weighed in a zoo.

Monkey A weighs 0.2 kg more than monkey B.
Monkey B weighs 4.1 kg.
Monkey C weighs 0.5 kg less than monkey D.
Monkey D weighs 0.5 kg more than monkey B.
Monkey E weighs 0.2 kg less than monkey B.

Which monkey weighs the most?

Three of the four words below are given in code.
The codes are not written in the same order as the words.
One of the codes is missing.

Mark the correct answers on the answer sheet.

| MEAT | DATE | MATE | SEAM |

5234   6425   5423

75. Find the code for the word **MATE**.

76. Find the code for the word **SAME**.

77. Find the word that has the number code **5263**.

78. Find the word that has the number code **4236**.

79. Find the word that has the number code **6345**.

80. Find the code for the word **SEAT**.

END OF TEST

Verbal Reasoning
Multiple-Choice
Practice Test C

Read these instructions carefully.

1. You must not open or turn over this booklet until you are told to do so.
2. The booklet is a multiple-choice test containing different types of questions.
3. Each question type begins with an explanation, usually followed by an example.
4. Do all rough working on a separate sheet of paper.
5. You should mark your answers in pencil on the answer sheet provided, not on this booklet.
6. You may have to mark more than one answer (you will be told this in the instructions for the question type). Draw a line firmly through the rectangle next to your answer.
7. Rub out any mistakes as well as you can and mark your new answer.
8. Try to do as many questions as you can. If you find that you cannot do a question, do not waste time on it but go on to the next one.
9. If you are stuck on a question, choose the answer that you think is best.
10. You have 50 minutes to complete the test.

In the following sets of five words, find the two words that are **different** from the rest. Mark them both on the answer sheet.

> Example: duck   goat   cow   swan   robin
> Answer: goat   cow

1. cylinder   rectangle   cone   cuboid   hexagon
2. furious   angry   upset   cross   hurt
3. tractor   truck   ferry   lorry   barge
4. boil   toast   oven   roast   pan
5. elude   run   avoid   jog   dodge
6. pronoun   apostrophe   comma   adverb   colon

In the following questions, take one letter from the word on the left and add it to the word on the right to make two new, proper words. The order of the letters within each word must not be changed. Mark the letter that moves on the answer sheet.

> Example: stand   ten
> Answer: t   (the two new words are 'sand' and 'tent')

7. breathe   prim
8. sight   sew
9. saviour   run
10. swoon   rap
11. fever   able
12. suave   sit

NOW GO ON TO THE NEXT PAGE

In the following questions, find the two words, one from each set, which will combine to make one new word, spelt correctly. You cannot change the order of the letters, and the word from the left-hand set always comes first. Mark both words on the answer sheet.

> **Example:** (back, behind, low)   (front, ground, above)
>
> **Answer:** back   ground   (the new word is 'background')

13. (fed, bud, lid)   (top, get, up)
14. (pave, road, cross)   (side, meant, sing)
15. (carp, year, ramp)   (page, post, age)
16. (suit, flaw, camp)   (ping, able, sight)
17. (tie, but, eat)   (knot, ton, up)
18. (stock, catch, count)   (out, king, pile)

In the following questions, choose one word from each set to best complete the sentences. Mark both words on the answer sheet, remembering to use one word from each set.

> **Example:** **Tall** is to (height, length, short) as **narrow** is to (wide, thin, road)
>
> **Answer:** short   wide

19. **Casual** is to (planned, informal, fancy) as **deliberate** is to (calculated, definite, suspicious).
20. **Teacher** is to (learn, school, student) as **major** is to (enemy, private, leader).
21. **Sensible** is to (prudent, clever, sensitive) as **extravagant** is to (exhausting, exceptional, excessive).
22. **Grass** is to (hedge, green, mow) as **food** is to (table, cook, fridge).
23. **Buckle** is to (belt, strap, hit) as **button** is to (needle, cuff, tie).
24. **Scalene** is to (circle, triangle, square) as **rhombus** is to (quadrilateral, sphere, symmetry).

NOW GO ON TO THE NEXT PAGE

In the following questions, the letters stand for numbers. Work out the answer to each sum as a letter and then mark it on the answer sheet.

> **Example:** If A = 2, B = 4, C = 5, D = 8, E = 12
> what is the answer to this sum written as a letter?
> B × C − E = ?
>
> **Answer:** D

25. If A = 30, B = 11, C = 15, D = 19, E = 27
what is the answer to this sum written as a letter?
A ÷ C × D − E = ?

26. If A = 3, B = 19, C = 12, D = 18, E = 20
what is the answer to this sum written as a letter?
A × C − B + A = ?

27. If A = 7, B = 9, C = 14, D = 22, E = 17
what is the answer to this sum written as a letter?
E − B + C = ?

28. If A = 17, B = 3, C = 94, D = 2, E = 9
what is the answer to this sum written as a letter?
D × A × B + E − C = ?

29. If A = 6, B = 18, C = 24, D = 12, E = 9
what is the answer to this sum written as a letter?
D × E ÷ A + B − D = ?

30. If A = 21, B = 13, C = 44, D = 7, E = 12
what is the answer to this sum written as a letter?
A ÷ D × E − B + A = ?

In the following sentences, a four-letter word is hidden across the end of one word and the start of the next word. Find the pair of words that contain the four-letter word and mark them on the answer sheet.

> **Example:** Richard ate his delicious breakfast hungrily.
>
> **Answer:** Richard **ate** (the hidden word is 'date')

31. Will you watch our new performance?
32. We watched the opera in London.
33. Seven times five add five is forty.
34. We collected money for the charity.
35. I banged my shin this morning.
36. The supporters did not act appropriately.

NOW GO ON TO THE NEXT PAGE

Find the number that will complete the sum correctly. Mark it on the answer sheet.

> **Example:** $5 + 8 = 6 + [?]$
>
> **Answer:** 7

37. $7 \times 9 - 44 = 57 \div [?]$
38. $120 \div 20 = 350 \div [?] - 44$
39. $15 \div 5 - 7 = 9 - [?]$
40. $11 - 4 + 8 = 28 \div [?] + 1$
41. $25 \times 3 \div 15 = 105 \div [?]$
42. $32 \div 16 \times 19 = 49 - [?]$

Read the information below and then use it to find the correct answer to the question. Mark the answer on the answer sheet.

43. Brendan, Phoebe, Luca, Orla and Javid share the same birthday. Brendan gets 5 birthday cards. Phoebe and Luca get more cards than Brendan. Javid gets twice as many cards as Orla. Orla gets 3 cards less than Brendan.

    If these statements are all true, only one of the sentences below **cannot** be true.
    Which one?
    A Phoebe gets 6 cards.
    B Luca gets the most cards.
    C Javid gets an odd number of cards.
    D All together, the children receive more than 20 cards.
    E Orla gets more than 1 card.

In the following sentences, one word written in capital letters has had three consecutive letters removed. These three missing letters make a three-letter word. Work out the three-letter word. Try out each of the options on the answer sheet to see which one works.

> **Example:** The **STER** scuttled into the corner of the cage.
>
> **Answer:** HAM   (the word in capitals is **HAMSTER**)

44. We had to **CEL** the trip due to bad weather.
45. Cathie **BEVES** every word her brother tells her.
46. Ciaran **SLED** his papers together.
47. The **HING** wind kept us awake all night.
48. In art today, we made **COLES** out of coloured foil.
49. Ronnie likes a glass of **MINL** water with his meals.

NOW GO ON TO THE NEXT PAGE

In the following questions, the three words on the right-hand side go together in the same way as the three words on the left-hand side. Work out the missing word and mark it on the answer sheet.

> **Example:** dark (yarn) nosy : pear (?) pool
>
> **Answer:** leap

50. stand (darn) risk : plods (?) lark
51. crash (slap) flop : wasps (?) bolt
52. sleep (plume) plums : tripe (?) glass
53. spin (dint) tend : flea (?) slat
54. free (fare) fear : lane (?) knew
55. crowd (draw) broad : thank (?) manic

In each question, there are two pairs of words. Select and mark a new word that goes **equally well** with both word pairs from the options on the answer sheet.

> **Example:** (firm, rigid)   (tricky, difficult)
>
> **Answer:** hard

56. (grade, assess)   (stain, blemish)
57. (aloof, cautious)   (booked, taken)
58. (blower, ventilator)   (admirer, follower)
59. (shoot, discharge)   (sack, dismiss)
60. (earth, ground)   (dirty, stain)
61. (push, squeeze)   (force, compel)

Read the information below and then use it to find the correct answer to the question. Mark the answer on the answer sheet.

62. Fred, Sonia, Bridie, Chen and Cal are 13, 12, 11, 11 and 9, but not in that order.
    Fred is 2 years younger than Sonia.
    Bridie is 3 years older than Chen.
    Chen is younger than Cal.
    Which two children are the same age?
    A Fred and Sonia
    B Sonia and Bridie
    C Bridie and Cal
    D Chen and Cal
    E Cal and Fred

In the following questions, some of the words are written in code. The first code word in each question is worked out for you. Using the same code, work out the second code word and mark it on the answer sheet. Remember that if you are working out a word created by the code, you will have to reverse the rule.

The alphabet is given here to help you.

A B C D E F G H I J K L M N O P Q R S T U V W X Y Z

> **Example:** If the code for **MELT** is **LDKS**, what is the code for **THAW**?
> **Answer:** SGZV

63. If the code for **SPIN** is **ROHM**, what is the code for **TURN**?

64. If the code for **CHAIR** is **DJDMW**, what is the code for **TABLE**?

65. If the code for **HIRE** is **IHSD**, what does **SDOS** mean?

66. If the code for **ELEPHANT** is **DIZIYPAE**, what is the code for **KANGAROO**?

67. If the code for **BIRD** is **DGTB**, what does **FMIQ** mean?

68. If the code for **DESSERT** is **XZOPCQT**, what is the code for **PUDDING**?

NOW GO ON TO THE NEXT PAGE

In the following questions, there are two sets of words. Choose the two words, one from each set, that are **closest** in meaning. Mark them both on the answer sheet.

> **Example:** (table, cup, knife)   (chair, fork, mug)
>
> **Answer:** cup   mug

69. (fly, spider, hurt)   (soar, web, scratch)
70. (flower, perfume, spray)   (plant, petal, scent)
71. (fantasy, report, enigma)   (mystery, fiction, genre)
72. (cautious, frivolous, wild)   (silly, wholesome, dutiful)
73. (stalk, brief, leave)   (hide, cover, pursue)
74. (nasty, incorrect, mediocre) (inappropriate, final, average)

The alphabet is given here to help you with the following questions.

A B C D E F G H I J K L M N O P Q R S T U V W X Y Z

In each question there is a series of letters following a pattern. Work out the pattern of the sequence and mark the correct pair of letters to continue the sequence on the answer sheet.

> **Example:** EW   FX   GY   HZ   ?
>
> **Answer:** IA

75. JV   HX   FZ   DB   ?
76. II   ME   RZ   XT   EM   ?
77. CB   ED   BC   DE   AD   ?
78. CY   ZD   WI   TN   QS   ?
79. KL   FQ   BU   YX   WZ   ?
80. AD   HY   CF   JA   EH   ?

END OF TEST

Verbal Reasoning
Multiple-Choice
Practice Test D

Read these instructions carefully.

1. You must not open or turn over this booklet until you are told to do so.

2. The booklet is a multiple-choice test containing different types of questions.

3. Each question type begins with an explanation, usually followed by an example.

4. Do all rough working on a separate sheet of paper.

5. You should mark your answers in pencil on the answer sheet provided, not on this booklet.

6. You may have to mark more than one answer (you will be told this in the instructions for the question type). Draw a line firmly through the rectangle next to your answer.

7. Rub out any mistakes as well as you can and mark your new answer.

8. Try to do as many questions as you can. If you find that you cannot do a question, do not waste time on it but go on to the next one.

9. If you are stuck on a question, choose the answer that you think is best.

10. You have 50 minutes to complete the test.

Find the word that completes the third pair of words in the same way as the first two pairs. Mark the word on the answer sheet.

> **Example:** (kite   kit)   (pipe   pip)   (seat [?])
> **Answer:** sea

1. (award   war)   (apart   par)   (board   [?])
2. (sword   row)   (spark   rap)   (spank   [?])
3. (honest   son)   (finest   sin)   (gobble   [?])
4. (smashed   ash)   (arrange   ran)   (weavers   [?])
5. (spin   nip)   (trap   par)   (care   [?])
6. (sloppy   lop)   (floaty   lot)   (corner   [?])

In the following questions, there are two sets of words. Choose the two words, one from each set, that are **closest** in meaning. Mark them both on the answer sheet.

> **Example:** (table, cup, knife)   (chair, fork, mug)
> **Answer:** cup   mug

7. (correct, phoney, peeved)   (authentic, technical, fake)
8. (chaos, hectic, fury)   (mayhem, suppression, prudence)
9. (faint, wholesome, haggard)   (gaunt, hefty, distinctive)
10. (spur, crave, captivate)   (whip, motivate, gallop)
11. (push, flog, snare)   (pull, thrash, break)
12. (resilient, different, cautious)   (haughty, vulnerable, tough)

NOW GO ON TO THE NEXT PAGE

In the following questions, the letters stand for numbers. Work out the answer to each sum as a letter and then mark it on the answer sheet.

> **Example:** If A = 2, B = 4, C = 5, D = 8, E = 12
> what is the answer to this sum written as a letter?
> B × C − E = ?
>
> **Answer:** D

13. If A = 25, B = 58, C = 5, D = 29, E = 87
    what is the answer to this sum written as a letter?
    A ÷ C × D − B = ?

14. If A = 7, B = 9, C = 12, D = 95, E = 20
    what is the answer to this sum written as a letter?
    A × C − B + E = ?

15. If A = 5, B = 4, C = 9, D = 125, E = 46
    what is the answer to this sum written as a letter?
    A × B × C − E − C = ?

16. If A = 10, B = 15, C = 20, D = 25, E = 30
    what is the answer to this sum written as a letter?
    E ÷ B × C − D = ?

17. If A = 19, B = 12, C = 36, D = 4, E = 29
    what is the answer to this sum written as a letter?
    A − B + E = ?

18. If A = 4, B = 23, C = 12, D = 8, E = 24
    what is the answer to this sum written as a letter?
    D × C ÷ A = ?

In the following questions, find the two words, one from each set, which will combine to make one new word, spelt correctly. You cannot change the order of the letters, and the word from the left-hand side always comes first. Mark both words on the answer sheet.

> **Example:** (back, behind, low)   (front, ground, above)
> **Answer:** back   ground   (the new word is 'background')

19. (leg, foot, arm)   (age, old, ankle)
20. (hedge, border, garden)   (bush, earth, row)
21. (computer, screen, key)   (bored, shot, door)
22. (thread, sew, needle)   (stitch, pin, bare)
23. (little, trouble, plenty)   (some, full, lot)
24. (hood, tab, tape)   (scarf, trick, let)

NOW GO ON TO THE NEXT PAGE

In the following questions, take one letter from the word on the left and add it to the word on the right to make two new, proper words. The order of the letters within each word must not be changed. Mark the letter that moves on the answer sheet.

Example: stand   ten
Answer: t   (the two new words are 'sand' and 'tent')

25. share   ire
26. chain   net
27. clout   pot
28. coast   tack
29. weary   what
30. pain   are

In the following questions, one letter can be used to end the first word and start the second word to make four new words. The same letter must be used to complete both pairs of words. Mark the letter on the answer sheet.

Example: LAM (?) ALE   SNO (?) ILL
Answer: B   (The four new words are LAMB, BALE, SNOB, BILL)

31. FO   (?) AIN   PEA (?) EAD
32. MAL (?) EAD   BAI (?) AWN
33. LOGI (?) ASH   AR (?) ARP
34. BAR (?) OTE   SO (?) APE
35. MEDI (?) WE   FLE (?) RGUE
36. BAI (?) OLL   SOU (?) EAST

Read the information below and then use it to find the correct answer to the question. Mark the colour on the answer sheet.

37. Abby, Jake, Stella, Ganesh and Chloe have to decide on the colour of T-shirt they will wear on sports day.
    Abby chooses blue.
    Jake will wear any colour apart from red, blue or green.
    Chloe will only wear white or yellow.
    Ganesh will wear yellow or red but not green, blue or white.
    Stella chooses green.
    Which colour T-shirt is most popular?

In the following sentences, a four-letter word is hidden across the end of one word and the start of the next word. Find the pair of words that contain the four-letter word and mark them on the answer sheet.

> **Example:** Richard ate his delicious breakfast hungrily.
>
> **Answer:** Richard ate (the hidden word is 'date')

38. My sister is two years old.

39. That's how Jamie always does it.

40. We discussed the play over breaktime.

41. Dad will need the car today.

42. I can't see you until later.

43. Mia is angry with me today.

In the following sentences, one word written in capital letters has had three letters removed. These three missing letters make a three-letter word. Work out the three-letter word. Try out each of the options on the answer sheet to see which one works.

> **Example:** The **STER** scuttled into the corner of the cage.
>
> **Answer:** HAM (the word in capitals is **HAMSTER**)

44. I can't **HOM** what you're saying.

45. Some thugs have **DALISED** the playground.

46. **DAS** can be found in the mountains of south central China.

47. Kim placed the cups on the **LVES**.

48. The diamonds **SPLED** under the lights.

49. Raj likes **SLE** food.

NOW GO ON TO THE NEXT PAGE

The three numbers in each group are related in the same way. Find the number that correctly completes the last group. Mark the number on the answer sheet.

> Example: (7 [3] 21)   (8 [4] 32)   (9 [?] 45)
> Answer: 5

50. (56 [7] 8)   (54 [6] 9)   (81 [?] 9)
51. (16 [2] 20)   (32 [5] 42)   (4 [?] 16)
52. (5 [8] 13)   (9 [12] 17)   (11 [?] 21)
53. (17 [11] 3)   (25 [13] 6)   (31 [?] 4)
54. (7 [21] 6)   (5 [25] 10)   (3 [?] 24)
55. (3 [6] 8)   (2 [5] 10)   (6 [?] 2)

The alphabet is given here to help you with the following questions.

A B C D E F G H I J K L M N O P Q R S T U V W X Y Z

Complete the second pair of letters in the same way as the first pair. Mark the correct letter pair on the answer sheet.

> Example: EL is to FM as TU is to ?
> Answer: UV

56. QL is to UB as SN is to ?
57. BL is to YO as JA is to ?
58. FF is to HB as LQ is to ?
59. ZX is to AC as VT is to ?
60. AZ is to CX as DW is to ?
61. BE is to GJ as AC is to ?

NOW GO ON TO THE NEXT PAGE

Read the information below and then use it to find the correct answer to the question. Mark the answer on the answer sheet.

62. Katie, Bilal, Pippa, Lottie and Zara are returning to the UK from various airports in Europe.

    Katie's flight took off 3 hours after Pippa's. Zara's flight left before the others, at 8:30am. Lottie's flight left after Bilal's but before Pippa's. Pippa's flight was supposed to leave at 10:25am but was delayed by 35 minutes. Bilal's flight lasted 3¾ hours and arrived in the UK at 12:45pm.

    If these statements are all true, only one of the sentences below must be **true**. Which one?

    A Lottie arrived back in the UK before the others.
    B Bilal arrived back in the UK after the others.
    C Pippa's flight left at 10:55am.
    D Zara had the longest flight.
    E Katie left at 2:00pm.

In the following questions, some of the words are written in code. The first code word in each question is worked out for you. Using the same code, work out the second code word and mark it on the answer sheet. Remember that if you are working out a word created by the code, you will have to reverse the rule.

The alphabet is given here to help you.

A B C D E F G H I J K L M N O P Q R S T U V W X Y Z

> **Example:** If the code for **MELT** is **LDKS**, what is the code for **THAW**?
> **Answer:** SGZV

63. If the code for **SNOW** is **QLMU**, what is the code for **RAIN**?

64. If the code for **HEDGE** is **GCACZ**, what does **OJXJO** mean?

65. If the code for **METAL** is **NDUZM**, what is the code for **COPPER**?

66. If the code for **SHEEP** is **VBHYS**, what is the code for **LAMB**?

67. If the code for **SPACE** is **HKZXV**, what is the code for **JUPITER**?

68. If the code for **MONTH** is **KKHLX**, what does **WAUJ** mean?

In the following sets of five words, find the two words that are **different** from the rest. Mark them both on the answer sheet.

> **Example:**   duck   goat   cow   swan   robin
> **Answer:**   goat   cow

69.	lizard	dog	crocodile	fox	snake
70.	stadium	arena	football	ground	rugby
71.	apple	onion	orange	pea	plum
72.	knife	cut	fork	mash	spoon
73.	snow	wind	rain	sunshine	sleet
74.	speak	listen	talk	chatter	hear

Three of the four words below are given in code.
The codes are not written in the same order as the words.
One of the codes is missing.

Mark the correct answers on the answer sheet.

PURE   POUR   ROOT   TORE

5332   2356   4156

75. Find the code for the word **TORE**.

76. Find the code for the word **PURE**.

77. Find the word that has the number code **4352**.

STOP   POTS   SHOT   STEP

1264   4321   1532

78. Find the code for the word **SHOT**.

79. Find the word that has the number code **4321**.

80. Find the word that has the number code **1432**.

END OF TEST

Collins

PRACTICE PAPERS

Answers and Explanations

Verbal Reasoning

Practice Test A: Answers and Explanations

1. **b**
   Take the **b** from **table** to make **tale**; add it to **lend** to make **blend**.
2. **p**
   Take the **p** from **spoil** to make **soil**; add it to **sank** to make **spank**.
3. **l**
   Take the **l** from **clap** to make **cap**; add it to **fail** to make **flail**.
4. **t**
   Take the **t** from **trusty** to make **rusty**; add it to **sigh** to make **sight**.
5. **e**
   Take the **e** from **wine** to make **win**; add it to **blow** to make **below**.
6. **o**
   Take the **o** from **moan** to make **man**; add it to **range** to make **orange**.

7. D because $3 \times 6 = 18$; $18 \div 2 = 9$; D = 9
8. B because $3 + 9 + 17 = 29$; $29 - 6 = 23$; B = 23
9. D because $5 \times 9 = 45$; $45 - 24 = 21$; D = 21
10. B because $36 \div 12 = 3$; $3 + 21 = 24$; B = 24
11. D because $44 \div 11 = 4$; $4 \times 13 = 52$; $52 - 20 = 32$; D = 32
12. B because $36 \div 12 = 3$; $3 \times 6 = 18$; $18 - 9 = 9$; B = 9

13. **tab** + **let** = tablet
    No other pairs make a proper word.
14. **near** + **by** = nearby
    No other pairs make a proper word.
15. **coup** + **led** = coupled
    No other pairs make a proper word.
16. **car** + **nation** = carnation
    No other pairs make a proper word.
17. **war** + **fare** = warfare
    No other pairs make a proper word.
18. **mess** + **age** = message
    No other pairs make a proper word.

19. **ATE** which is missing from CONCENTRATED
20. **ERA** which is missing from SEVERAL
21. **CAP** which is missing from ESCAPED
22. **INK** which is missing from SPRINKLING
23. **ACT** which is missing from REACTED
24. **DEN** which is missing from ACCIDENTALLY

25. **TH** because the pattern of the initial letter in each pair is: J, L, N, P, R, which is + 2 each time; R + 2 = T. The pattern of the second letter in each pair is: C, D, E, F, G, which is + 1 each time; G + 1 = H.
26. **EY** because the pattern of the initial letter in each pair is: T, Q, N, K, H, which is − 3 each time; H − 3 = E. The pattern of the second letter in each pair is: J, M, P, S, V, which is + 3 each time; V + 3 = Y.
27. **VI** because the pattern of the initial letter in each pair is: R, V, A, G, N, which is + 4, + 5, + 6, + 7; N + 8 = V. The pattern of the second letter in each pair is: M, I, D, X, Q, which is − 4, − 5, − 6, − 7; Q − 8 = I.
28. **CH** because the pattern of the initial letter in each pair is: C, E, F, F, E, which is + 2, + 1, 0, − 1; E − 2 = C. The pattern of the second letter in each pair is: H, F, E, E, F, which is − 2, − 1, 0, + 1; F + 2 = H.

29. **NG** because the pattern of the initial letter in each pair is: C, B, Z, W, S, which is − 1, − 2, − 3, − 4; S − 5 = N. The pattern of the second letter in each pair is: C, E, D, F, E, which is + 2, − 1, + 2, − 1; E + 2 = G.
30. **DL** because the pattern of the initial letter in each pair is: D, F, C, E, B, which is + 2, − 3, + 2, − 3; B + 2 = D. The pattern of the second letter in each pair is: Q, N, P, M, O, which is − 3, + 2, − 3, + 2; O − 3 = L.

31. **C**
    A – we do not know if Carla is a farmer, just that she lives in the countryside.
    B – we know she has a red sports car but that doesn't mean she doesn't like other colours.
    D – just because Carla lives in the countryside doesn't mean she likes the countryside.
    E – just because she has a car and a van doesn't mean she likes cars and vans.

    C – We do know that Carla has at least two vehicles – a sports car and a van.

32. **relaxed** and **stressed** are opposite in meaning.
33. **reveal** and **conceal** are opposite in meaning.
34. **blunt** and **sharp** are opposite in meaning.
35. **loyal** and **unreliable** are opposite in meaning.
36. **obscure** and **clear** are opposite in meaning.
37. **wealthy** and **needy** are opposite in meaning.

38. **herd** from teac**her d**elivered
39. **sour** from That'**s our**
40. **epic** from th**e pic**nic
41. **shot** from i**s hot**ter
42. **stop** from be**st op**eratic
43. **them** from **the m**atch

44. 46
    Rule: + 9 each time
45. 37
    Rule: + 1, + 2, + 3, + 4, + 5
46. 5
    Rule: − 6, − 5, − 4, − 3, − 2, − 1
47. 35
    Rule: − 1, − 3, − 5, − 7, − 9, − 11. Subtract odd numbers.
48. 6
    Rule: alternate numbers: ÷ 2, interim numbers − 4
49. 46
    Rule: − 9, − 12, − 15, − 18, − 21. Subtract 3 more than the previous number.

50. **A**
    B – Ewan has 1 goldfish and 1 hamster = 2 pets; Brogan has 1 cat, 1 dog and 2 lizards = 4 pets. So, Ewan does not have more pets than Brogan.
    C – Sophie has 2 rabbits, 2 goldfish and 1 gerbil. She does not have a lizard.
    D – Brogan has only 1 dog.
    E – Joe has 1 hamster, Ewan has 1 hamster.

    A – Joe has 3 pets; Ewan has 2 pets; Brogan has 4 pets; Sophie has 5 pets, which is the most.

51. R
    SEVER, REND, BEAVER, REACH
52. H
    BLEACH, HEAVE, SIGH, HOLD
53. K
    WICK, KIND, SLICK, KNOT
54. A
    FLOTILLA, AMBLE, YOGA, AVENGE
55. L
    CAMEL, LAUNCH, YELL, LOAN
56. T
    CLOSET, THORN, SPENT, TURRET
57. HC because the rule for MQ to LP is − 1, − 1.
    I − 1 = H, D − 1 = C.
58. UZ because the rule for JP to LS is + 2, + 3.
    S + 2 = U, W + 3 = Z.
59. NC because the rule for QZ to MD is − 4, + 4.
    R − 4 = N, Y + 4 = C.
60. ZC because the rule for BY to WF is − 5, + 7.
    E − 5 = Z, V + 7 = C.
61. GT because the rule for AZ to FU is + 5, − 5.
    B + 5 = G, Y − 5 = T.
62. ZL because the rule for BG to KA is + 9, − 6.
    Q + 9 = Z, R − 6 = L.
63. **roll** can mean to revolve or turn or can refer to a bread bun.
64. **spot** can mean to observe/notice or can refer to a mark/stain.
65. **scale** can mean to climb up or over something, or refer to the size or extent of something.
66. **tender** can mean caring or refer to a part of the body that is painful when touched.
67. A **sling** can be a loop or band that supports or lifts something. It can also mean to throw something carelessly.
68. **dear** can mean something that is loved or something that is overpriced/expensive.
69. **let** because **pod** is made from the 1st and 2nd letter of the left-hand word and the 3rd letter of the right-hand word. **Let** is made the same way.
70. **fat** because **bar** is made from the 1st letter of the right-hand word, the 3rd letter of the left-hand word and the 2nd letter of the left-hand word. **Fat** is made the same way.
71. **mope** because **dine** is made from the 4th letter of the right-hand word, the 3rd letter of the left-hand word, the 4th letter of the left-hand word and the 2nd letter of the right-hand word. **Mope** is made the same way.
72. **silk** because **flap** is made from the 1st letter of the left-hand word, the 2nd letter of the right-hand word, the 3rd letter of the right-hand word and the 1st letter of the right-hand word. **Silk** is made the same way.
73. **milk** because **dine** is made from the 4th letter of the left-hand word, the 2nd letter of the left-hand word, the 3rd letter of the left-hand word and the 5th letter of the right-hand word. **Milk** is made the same way.
74. **prod** because **fret** is made from the 1st letter of the left-hand word, the 4th letter of the left-hand word, the 2nd letter of the right-hand word and the 4th letter of the right-hand word. **Prod** is made the same way.
75. **undertake** and **continue** because the rest mean to join forces or work together.
76. **France** and **Italy** because the rest are continents.
77. **tornado** and **hurricane** because the rest are associated with wet weather but not necessarily wind.
78. **nylon** and **plastic** because the rest are natural materials.
79. **goldfish** and **crow** because the rest are amphibians.
80. **moist** and **wet** because the rest are associated with lack of water.

Practice Test B: Answers and Explanations

1. **crime** and **offence** as no other pair is close in meaning.
2. **stumble** and **stagger** as no other pair is close in meaning.
3. **delicate** and **fragile** as no other pair is close in meaning.
4. **succumb** and **surrender** as no other pair is close in meaning.
5. **aspect** and **feature** as no other pair is close in meaning.
6. **blatant** and **obvious** as no other pair is close in meaning.

7. **scar** from like**s car**ing
8. **none** from tha**n one**
9. **they** from **the y**oung
10. **stun** from be**st un**iform
11. **stab** from ju**st ab**out
12. **also** from fin**al so**ng

13. l
    Take the l from **blank** to make **bank**; add it to **band** to make **bland**.
14. t
    Take the t from **there** to make **here**; add it to **sore** to make **store**.
15. c
    Take the c from **batch** to make **bath**; add it to **lip** to make **clip**.
16. a
    Take the a from **taint** to make **tint**; add it to **pint** to make **paint**.
17. s
    Take the s from **jest** to make **jet**; add it to **and** to make **sand**.
18. t
    Take the t from **teach** to make **each**; add it to **ear** to make **tear**.

19. 8
    Subtract the third number from the first number.
20. 22
    Subtract the first number from the third number.
21. 9
    Add the two outer numbers, then divide the answer by 2.
22. 39
    Add the two outer numbers, then subtract 2 from the answer.
23. 26
    Add the two outer numbers, then double the answer.
24. 18
    Divide the first number by the third number. Multiply the answer by 3.

25. **write** and **sign** because the rest are reading materials.
26. **light** and **switch** because the rest are types of furniture.
27. **high jump** and **hurdles** because the rest are team sports played with a ball.
28. **cube** and **sphere** because the rest are 2D shapes.
29. **recover** and **find** because the rest relate to following.
30. **eye** and **ear** because the rest are senses.

31. **PQKUG** because SPEAK = URGCM where the rule is + 2 letters.
    N + 2 = P, O + 2 = Q, I + 2 = K, S + 2 = U, E + 2 = G
32. **BIN** because LOG = KNF where the rule is − 1 letter.
    AHM: you need to reverse the rule so + 1 letter each time.
    A + 1 = B, H + 1 = I, M + 1 = N
33. **NQDR** because BITE = CKWI where the rule is + 1, + 2, + 3, + 4.
    M + 1 = N, O + 2 = Q, A + 3 = D, N + 4 = R
34. **PLAN** because SINK = QKLM where the rule is − 2, + 2 each time.
    NNYP: you need to reverse the rule so + 2, − 2 each time.
    N + 2 = P, N − 2 = L, Y + 2 = A, P − 2 = N
35. **PWIX** because BLOW = YHJQ where the rule is − 3, − 4, − 5, − 6.
    S − 3 = P, A − 4 = W, N − 5 = I, D − 6 = X
36. **FOZR** because BLUE = AIPX where the rule is − 1, − 3, − 5, − 7
    G − 1 = F, R − 3 = O, E − 5 = Z, Y − 7 = R

37. 17
    27 + 18 = 45
    62 − 17 = 45
38. 9
    15 − 7 = 8
    72 ÷ 9 = 8
39. 9
    5 × 3 = 15; 15 + 12 = 27; 27 − 4 = 23
    32 − 9 = 23
40. 39
    18 ÷ 3 = 6; 6 × 7 = 42
    9^2 = 81; 81 − 39 = 42
41. 28
    49 ÷ 7 = 7; 7 × 8 = 56; 56 − 5 = 51
    100 − 77 = 23; 23 + 28 = 51
42. 61
    12 × 9 = 108; 108 ÷ 3 = 36; 36 − 17 = 19
    4 × 20 = 80; 80 − 61 = 19

43. 2
    Rajiv brings sandwiches and fruit.
    Cameron brings crisps and pizza.
    Abby brings pizza and juice.
    George brings sandwiches, fruit, pizza and juice.
    Lizzie brings pizza, juice, sandwiches and fruit.
    So, three children bring sandwiches, which means two do not.

44. **sky, ocean**
    Stars are to sky as fish are to ocean because they are places where they are found.
45. **ate, had**
    Eat is to ate as have is to had because both are the past tenses.
46. **three, eight**
    Triangle is to three as octagon is to eight because both are the number of sides (and vertices) that each have.
47. **stalk, trunk**
    Leaf is to stalk as branch is to trunk because a leaf is attached to a stalk and a branch is attached to a trunk.
48. **listen, watch**
    Radio is to listen as film is to watch because you listen to the radio and you watch a film.

49. **rocket, ship**
    Astronaut is to rocket as captain is to ship because both are their modes of transport.
50. **are** because **tin** and **nor** are made from the middle three letters of stint and snore. **Are** is made the same way.
51. **sling** because **spend** and **fling** are made from the 1st, 4th, 5th, 6th and 7th letters of suspend and feeling. **Sling** is made the same way.
52. **bar** because **fin** and **sea** are made from the 1st, 3rd and 4th letters of faint and swear. **Bar** is made the same way.
53. **era** because **toy** and **key** are made from the 5th, 3rd and 6th letters of floaty and cheeky. **Era** is made the same way.
54. **eat** because **son** and **sin** are made from the 5th, 2nd and 3rd letters of honest and finest. **Eat** is made the same way.
55. **tuna** because **draw** and **debt** are made from the 6th, 5th, 4th and 3rd letters of reward and hotbed. **Tuna** is made the same way.
56. 21
    Rule: add the two previous numbers to get the next number in the sequence. $2 + 3 = 5$; $3 + 5 = 8$; $5 + 8 = 13$; $8 + 13 = 21$
57. 5
    Rule: $- 17, - 16, - 15, - 14, - 13$
58. 261
    Rule: $+ 77$ each time.
59. 15
    Rule: alternate numbers are the result of the interim squared numbers minus 1.
60. 42
    Rule: alternate numbers are the same for two, then $+ 1$ for the next two; interim numbers increase by 6 each time.
61. 88
    Rule: $- 8$ each time.
62. **ant** + **hem** = anthem
    No other words make a proper word.
63. **water** + **side** = waterside
    No other words make a proper word.
64. **scar** + **let** = scarlet
    No other words make a proper word.
65. **pump** + **kin** = pumpkin
    No other words make a proper word.
66. **god** + **send** = godsend
    No other words make a proper word.
67. **alter** + **native** = alternative
    No other words make a proper word.
68. **CON** which is missing from CONDITION
69. **RIB** which is missing from DESCRIBE
70. **SEA** which is missing from RESEARCH
71. **TEN** which is missing from PRETENDING
72. **RAN** which is missing from TRANSLATED
73. **ASH** which is missing from WASHING
74. D
    Monkey A weighs $4.1 + 0.2 = 4.3$ kg
    Monkey B weighs 4.1 kg
    Monkey C weighs $4.6 - 0.5 = 4.1$ kg
    Monkey D weighs $4.1 + 0.5 = 4.6$ kg
    Monkey E weighs $4.1 - 0.2 = 3.9$ kg
    So Monkey D weighs the most.
75. 5234
76. 6254
77. MAST
78. EATS
79. STEM
80. 6423

Practice Test C: Answers and Explanations

1. **Rectangle** and **hexagon** because the rest are 3D shapes.
2. **Upset** and **hurt** because the rest mean angry.
3. **Ferry** and **barge** because the rest are road vehicles.
4. **Oven** and **pan** because the rest are cooking methods.
5. **Run** and **jog** because the rest refer to avoiding something.
6. **Pronoun** and **adverb** because the rest are punctuation marks.
7. e
   Take the **e** from **breathe** to make **breath**; add it to **prim** to make **prime**.
8. t
   Take the **t** from **sight** to make **sigh**; add it to **sew** to make **stew**.
9. i
   Take the **i** from **saviour** to make **savour**; add it to **run** to make **ruin**.
10. w
    Take the **w** from **swoon** to make **soon**; add it to **rap** to make **wrap**.
11. f
    Take the **f** from **fever** to make **ever**; add it to **able** to make **fable**.
12. u
    Take the **u** from **suave** to make **save**; add it to **sit** to make **suit**.
13. **bud** + **get** = budget
    No other words make a proper word.
14. **road** + **side** = roadside
    No other words make a proper word.
15. **ramp** + **age** = rampage
    No other words make a proper word.
16. **suit** + **able** = suitable
    No other words make a proper word.
17. **but** + **ton** = button
    No other words make a proper word.
18. **stock** + **pile** = stockpile
    No other words make a proper word.
19. informal, calculated
    Casual is to informal as deliberate is to calculated because informal is a synonym for casual and calculated is a synonym for deliberate.
20. student, private
    Teacher is to student as major is to private because a student is subordinate to a teacher and a private is subordinate to a major.
21. prudent, excessive
    Sensible is to prudent as extravagant is to excessive because prudent is a synonym for sensible and excessive is a synonym for extravagant.
22. mow, cook
    Grass is to mow as food is to cook because mow is something you do to grass and cook is something you do to food.
23. belt, cuff
    Buckle is to belt as button is to cuff because they are both types of fastenings.
24. triangle, quadrilateral
    Scalene is to triangle as rhombus is to quadrilateral because a scalene is a type of triangle and a rhombus is a type of quadrilateral.
25. B because $30 \div 15 = 2$; $2 \times 19 = 38$; $38 - 27 = 11$; B = 11
26. E because $3 \times 12 = 36$; $36 - 19 = 17$; $17 + 3 = 20$; E = 20
27. D because $17 - 9 = 8$; $8 + 14 = 22$; D = 22
28. A because $2 \times 17 \times 3 = 102$; $102 + 9 = 111$; $111 - 94 = 17$; A = 17
29. C because $12 \times 9 = 108$; $108 \div 6 = 18$; $18 + 18 = 36$; $36 - 12 = 24$; C = 24
30. C because $21 \div 7 = 3$; $3 \times 12 = 36$; $36 - 13 = 23$; $23 + 21 = 44$; C = 44

31. **hour** from watch **our**
32. **rain** from opera **in**
33. **vent** from Seven times
34. **fort** from **for** the
35. **hint** from shin this
36. **tact** from not act

37. 3
    $7 \times 9 = 63$; $63 - 44 = 19$
    $57 \div 3 = 19$
38. 7
    $120 \div 20 = 6$
    $350 \div 7 = 50$; $50 - 44 = 6$
39. 13
    $15 \div 5 = 3$; $3 - 7 = -4$
    $9 - 13 = -4$
40. 2
    $11 - 4 = 7$; $7 + 8 = 15$
    $28 \div 2 = 14$; $14 + 1 = 15$
41. 21
    $25 \times 3 = 75$; $75 \div 15 = 5$
    $105 \div 21 = 5$
42. 11
    $32 \div 16 = 2$; $2 \times 19 = 38$
    $49 - 11 = 38$

43. C
    Brendan gets 5 cards and Orla gets 3 less than him so that means she gets 2 cards; if Javid gets twice as many as Orla, then he receives 4 cards, which is an even number so sentence C **cannot** be true. We don't know exactly how many cards Phoebe and Luca get, so we don't know for sure if A and B are true or not.

44. CAN which is missing from CANCEL.
45. LIE which is missing from BELIEVES.
46. TAP which is missing from STAPLED.
47. OWL which is missing from HOWLING.
48. LAG which is missing from COLLAGES.
49. ERA which is missing from MINERAL.

50. **sold** because **darn** is made from last the letter of the left-hand word, the 3rd letter of left-hand word, the first letter of the right-hand word and the 4th letter of the left-hand word. **Sold** is made the same way.
51. **post** because **slap** is made from the 4th letter of the left-hand word, the 2nd letter of right-hand word, the 3rd letter of the left-hand word and the last letter of the right-hand word. **Post** is made the same way.
52. **grasp** because **plume** is made from the first letter of the right-hand word, the 2nd letter of the left-hand word,

the 3rd and 4th letters of the right-hand word and the 4th letter of the left-hand word. **Grasp** is made the same way.

53. **teas** because **dint** is made from the 4th letter of the right-hand word, the 3rd letter of the left-hand word, the 4th letter of the left-hand word (or the 3rd letter of the right-hand word) and the first letter of the right-hand word. **Teas** is made the same way.
54. **lean** because **fare** is made from the first letter of the left-hand word, the 3rd letter of the right-hand word, the 2nd letter of the left-hand word and the 2nd letter of the right-hand word (or the 3rd letter of the left-hand word). **Lean** is made the same way.
55. **chin** because **draw** is made from the last letter of the right-hand word, the 2nd letter of the left-hand word, the 4th letter of the right-hand word and the 4th letter of the left-hand word. **Chin** is made the same way.
56. **mark** can mean to give a grade to or assess a piece of work, or can refer to a stain.
57. **reserved** can describe someone who is distant or unsociable or something that is held for future use, e.g. a table in a restaurant.
58. **fan** can mean something that blows air or someone who admires or is devoted to someone.
59. **fire** can mean to shoot, or it can be used informally meaning to dismiss from a job.
60. **soil** can mean earth or ground (such as in the garden), or to dirty something.
61. **press** can mean to push or squeeze, or to force or compel someone to do something.
62. E
    Cal and Fred are both 11 years old.
    If Bridie is 3 years older than Chen, she must be 12 and he must be 9 as they are the only ages with a three-year gap. If Fred is 2 years younger than Sonia, he must be 11 and Sonia must be 13. We are then left with another 11-year-old, which must be Cal as Chen is younger than Cal.
63. **STQM** because SPIN = ROHM where the rule is − 1 letter.
    T − 1 = S, U − 1 = T, R − 1 = Q, N − 1 = M
64. **UCEPJ** because CHAIR = DJDMW where the rule is + 1, + 2, + 3, + 4, + 5.
    T + 1 = U, A + 2 = C, B + 3 = E, L + 4 = P, E + 5 = J
65. **RENT** because HIRE = IHSD where the rule is + 1, − 1 each time.
    SDOS: you need to reverse the rule so − 1, + 1 each time.
    S − 1 = R, D + 1 = E, O − 1 = N, S + 1 = T
66. **JXIZRGBZ** because ELEPHANT = DIZIYPAE where the rule is −1, −3, −5, −7, −9, −11, − 13, −15.
    K − 1 = J, A − 3 = X, N − 5 = I, G − 7 = Z, A − 9 = R, R − 11 = G, O − 13 = B, O − 15 = Z
67. **DOGS** because BIRD = DGTB where the rule is + 2, − 2 each time.
    FMIQ: you need to reverse the rule so − 2, + 2 each time.
    F − 2 = D, M + 2 = O, I − 2 = G, Q + 2 = S
68. **JPZAGMG** because DESSERT = XZOPCQT where the rule is − 6, − 5, − 4, − 3, − 2, − 1, 0.
    P − 6 = J, U − 5 = P, D − 4 = Z, D − 3 = A, I − 2 = G, N − 1 = M, G = G
69. **fly** and **soar** as no other pair is close in meaning.
70. **perfume** and **scent** as no other pair is close in meaning.
71. **enigma** and **mystery** as no other pair is close in meaning.
72. **frivolous** and **silly** as no other pair is close in meaning.
73. **stalk** and **pursue** as no other pair is close in meaning.
74. **mediocre** and **average** as no other pair is close in meaning.
75. **BD** because the pattern of the initial letter in each pair is: J, H, F, D, which is − 2 each time; D − 2 = B. The pattern of the second letter in each pair is: V, X, Z, B, which is + 2 each time; B + 2 = D.
76. **ME** because the pattern of the initial letter in each pair is: I, M, R, X, E which is + 4, + 5, + 6, + 7; E + 8 = M. The pattern of the second letter in each pair is: I, E, Z, T, M which is − 4, − 5, − 6, − 7; M − 8 = E.
77. **CF** because the pattern of the initial letter in each pair is: C, E, B, D, A, which is + 2, − 3, + 2, − 3; A + 2 = C. The pattern of the second letter in each pair is: B, D, C, E, D, which is + 2, − 1, + 2, − 1; D + 2 = F.
78. **NX** because the pattern of the initial letter in each pair is: C, Z, W, T, Q, which is − 3 each time; Q − 3 = N. The pattern of the second letter in each pair is: Y, D, I, N, S, which is + 5 each time. S + 5 = X.
79. **VA** because the pattern of the initial letter in each pair is: K, F, B, Y, W, which is − 5, − 4, − 3, − 2; W − 1 = V. The pattern of the second letter in each pair is: L, Q, U, X, Z, which is + 5, + 4, + 3, + 2; Z + 1 = A.
80. **LC** because the pattern of the initial letter in each pair is: A, H, C, J, E, which is + 7, − 5, + 7, − 5; E + 7 = L. The pattern of the second letter in each pair is: D, Y, F, A, H, which is − 5, + 7, − 5, + 7; H − 5 = C.

Practice Test D: Answers and Explanations

1. **oar** because **war** and **par** are made from the 2nd, 3rd and 4th letters of award and apart. **Oar** is made the same way.
2. **nap** because **row** and **rap** are made from the 4th, 3rd and 2nd letters of sword and spark. **Nap** is made the same way.
3. **lob** because **son** and **sin** are made from the 5th, 2nd and 3rd letters of honest and finest. **Lob** is made the same way.
4. **awe** because **ash** and **ran** are made from the 3rd, 1st and 5th letters of smashed and arrange. **Awe** is made the same way.
5. **era** because **nip** and **par** are made from the 4th, 3rd and 2nd letters of spin and trap. **Era** is made the same way.
6. **ore** because **lop** and **lot** are made from the 2nd, 3rd and 5th letters of sloppy and floaty. **Ore** is made the same way.
7. **phoney** and **fake** as no other pair is close in meaning.
8. **chaos** and **mayhem** as no other pair is close in meaning.
9. **haggard** and **gaunt** as no other pair is close in meaning.
10. **spur** and **motivate** as no other pair is close in meaning.
11. **flog** and **thrash** as no other pair is close in meaning.
12. **resilient** and **tough** as no other pair is close in meaning.
13. E because $25 \div 5 = 5$; $5 \times 29 = 145$; $145 - 58 = 87$; E = 87
14. D because $7 \times 12 = 84$; $84 - 9 = 75$; $75 + 20 = 95$; D = 95
15. D because $5 \times 4 \times 9 = 180$; $180 - 46 = 134$; $134 - 9 = 125$; D = 125
16. B because $30 \div 15 = 2$; $2 \times 20 = 40$; $40 - 25 = 15$; B = 15
17. C because $19 - 12 = 7$; $7 + 29 = 36$; C = 36
18. E because $8 \times 12 = 96$; $96 \div 4 = 24$; E = 24
19. **foot** + **age** = footage
    No other pairs make a proper word.
20. **hedge** + **row** = hedgerow
    No other pairs make a proper word.
21. **screen** + **shot** = screenshot
    No other pairs make a proper word.
22. **thread** + **bare** = threadbare
    No other pairs make a proper word.
23. **trouble** + **some** = troublesome
    No other pairs make a proper word.
24. **tab** + **let** = tablet
    No other pairs make a proper word.
25. **s**
    Take the **s** from **share** to make **hare**; add it to **ire** to make **sire**.
26. **a**
    Take the **a** from **chain** to make **chin**; add it to **net** to make **neat**.
27. **u**
    Take the **u** from **clout** to make **clot**; add it to **pot** to make **pout**.
28. **s**
    Take the **s** from **coast** to make **coat**; add it to **tack** to make **stack** or **tacks**.

29. **e**
    Take the **e** from **weary** to make **wary**; add it to **what** to make **wheat**.
30. **a**
    Take the **a** from **pain** to make **pin**; add it to **are** to make **area**.
31. **R**
    FOR, RAIN, PEAR, READ
32. **L**
    MALL, LEAD, BAIL, LAWN
33. **C**
    LOGIC, CASH, ARC, CARP
34. **N**
    BARN, NOTE, SON, NAPE
35. **A**
    MEDIA, AWE, FLEA, ARGUE
36. **L**
    BAIL, LOLL, SOUL, LEAST

37. **Yellow**
    Abby – blue; Jake – yellow or white; Stella – green; Ganesh – yellow or red; Chloe – yellow or white. As yellow appears three times, it is the most popular colour.

38. **sold** from year**s old**.
39. **show** from That'**s how**.
40. **verb** from o**ver b**reaktime.
41. **cart** from **car t**oday.
42. **till** from un**til l**ater.
43. **sang** from i**s ang**ry.

44. **FAT** which is missing from FATHOM
45. **VAN** which is missing from VANDALISED
46. **PAN** which is missing from PANDAS
47. **SHE** which is missing from SHELVES
48. **ARK** which is missing from SPARKLED
49. **IMP** which is missing from SIMPLE

50. 9
    Divide the 1st number by the 3rd number.
51. 6
    Subtract the 1st number from the 3rd number and halve the answer.
52. 15
    Add the 1st number and the 3rd number, divide answer by 2, then subtract 1.
53. 23
    Multiply the 3rd number by 2. Subtract the answer from the 1st number.
54. 36
    Halve the 3rd number and multiply the answer by the 1st number.
55. 3
    Multiply the two outer numbers and divide the answer by 4.

56. **WD** because the rule for QL to UB is $+ 4, - 10$.
    $S + 4 = W$. $N - 10 = D$.
57. **GD** because the rule for BL to YO is $- 3, + 3$.
    $J - 3 = G$. $A + 3 = D$.
58. **NM** because the rule for FF to HB is $+2, -4$.
    $L + 2 = N$. $Q - 4 = M$.

59. **WY** because the rule for ZX to AC is + 1, + 5.
    V + 1 = W. T + 5 = Y.
60. **FU** because the rule for AZ to CX is + 2, – 2. D + 2 = F.
    W – 2 = U.
61. **FH** because the rule for BE to GJ is +5. A + 5 = F.
    C + 5 = H.
62. **E**
    Pippa's flight was delayed by 35 minutes so she departed at 11.00am. If Katie's flight took off 3 hours later, she must have left at 2.00pm.
63. **PYGL** because SNOW = QLMU where the rule is – 2 letters.
    R – 2 = P, A – 2 = Y, I – 2 = G, N – 2 = L.
64. **PLANT** because HEDGE = GCACZ where the rule is – 1, – 2, – 3, – 4, – 5.
    OJXJO: you need to reverse the rule so + 1, + 2, + 3, + 4, + 5.
    O + 1 = P, J + 2 = L, X + 3 = A, J + 4 = N, O + 5 = T.
65. **DNQOFQ** because METAL = NDUZM where the rule is + 1, – 1.
    C + 1 = D, O – 1 = N, P + 1 = Q, P – 1 = O, E + 1 = F, R – 1 = Q.
66. **OUPV** because SHEEP = VBHYS where the rule is + 3, – 6.
    L + 3 = O, A – 6 = U, M + 3 = P, B – 6 = V.
67. **QFKRGVI** because HKZXV is the mirror code for SPACE. QFKRGVI is the mirror code for JUPITER.
68. **YEAR** because MONTH = KKHLX where the rule is – 2, – 4, – 6, – 8, – 10.
    WAUJ: you need to reverse the rule so + 2, + 4, + 6, + 8.
    W + 2 = Y, A + 4 = E, U + 6 = A, J + 8 = R.
69. **dog** and **fox** because the others have scales/are reptiles.
70. **football** and **rugby** because the others are where sports take place.
71. **onion** and **pea** because the others are fruits.
72. **cut** and **mash** because the others are utensils.
73. **wind** and **sunshine** because the others are types of 'wet' weather.
74. **listen** and **hear** because the others are things that we do with our mouths.
75. **2356**
76. **4156**
77. **PORT**
78. **1532**
79. **POTS**
80. **SPOT**

Notes

Notes

Notes

VERBAL REASONING TEST A

VR A

Pupil's Name:
School Name:
Date of Test:

PUPIL NUMBER / **SCHOOL NUMBER** / **DATE OF BIRTH**

Please mark like this ⊟.

EXAMPLE
- s
- t
- a
- n
- d

1.
- t
- a
- b
- l
- e

2.
- s
- p
- o
- i
- l

3.
- c
- l
- a
- p

4.
- t
- r
- u
- s
- t
- y

5.
- w
- i
- n
- e

6.
- m
- o
- a
- n

EXAMPLE
- A
- B
- C
- D
- E

7. A B C D E
8. A B C D E
9. A B C D E
10. A B C D E
11. A B C D E
12. A B C D E

EXAMPLE
- back — front
- behind — ground
- low — above

13.
- cup — free
- hope — let
- tab — full

14.
- near — off
- far — in
- out — by

15.
- date — led
- coup — fruit
- fast — mouse

16.
- truck — nation
- car — rage
- van — wheel

17.
- wide — down
- war — fare
- scroll — world

18.
- mess — age
- tell — tail
- miss — time

EXAMPLE
- EEL
- CON
- VIM
- HAM
- RUN

19.
- TEN
- ATE
- RED
- EAT
- NET

20.
- ERA
- ELF
- EAR
- SET
- VAN

21.
- SAP
- PAT
- CAP
- CAT
- RED

22.
- ARK
- ART
- OWL
- INK
- TOW

23.
- CAT
- ERA
- LED
- FUR
- ACT

24.
- DAB
- DEN
- TEN
- TEA
- PEN

EXAMPLE
- IB
- HI
- HA
- IA
- IY

25.
- SH
- EY
- TH
- EX
- EW

26.
- IP
- GR
- FT
- EY
- JR

27.
- VI
- WJ
- VJ
- WH
- UI

28.
- BI
- CH
- CI
- DH
- CD

29.
- MF
- NF
- OP
- OF
- NG

30.
- AP
- DL
- DM
- EL
- FE

31.
- A
- B
- C
- D
- E

© HarperCollins Publishers Ltd

VR A

PUPIL NUMBER

[0] [0] [0] [0] [0] [0]
[1] [1] [1] [1] [1] [1]
[2] [2] [2] [2] [2] [2]
[3] [3] [3] [3] [3] [3]
[4] [4] [4] [4] [4] [4]
[5] [5] [5] [5] [5] [5]
[6] [6] [6] [6] [6] [6]
[7] [7] [7] [7] [7] [7]
[8] [8] [8] [8] [8] [8]
[9] [9] [9] [9] [9] [9]

EXAMPLE
- late
- morning
- breakfast
- bed
- early
- time

32
- fierce
- smooth
- relaxed
- stressed
- calmly
- silky

33
- reveal
- regard
- observe
- find
- excavate
- conceal

34
- pencil
- blunt
- nib
- pen
- sharp
- lead

35
- loyal
- faithless
- promise
- keep
- pretence
- unreliable

36
- slight
- transparent
- obscure
- power
- clear
- helpless

37
- royal
- wealthy
- scant
- needy
- fulfilled
- safe

EXAMPLE
- Richard ate
- ate his
- his delicious
- delicious breakfast
- breakfast hungrily

38
- The teacher
- teacher delivered
- delivered a
- a great
- great lesson

39
- That's our
- our aunt's
- aunt's house
- house on
- on the
- the corner

40
- Please come
- come to
- to the
- the picnic
- picnic tomorrow

41
- Today is
- is hotter
- hotter than
- than it
- it was
- was yesterday

42
- It was
- was the
- the best
- best operatic
- operatic performance
- performance ever

43
- We went
- went home
- home after
- after the
- the match

EXAMPLE
- 9
- 12
- 13
- 15
- 18

44: 56, 52, 46, 45, 49

45: 37, 39, 33, 38, 41

46: 7, 9, 11, 5, 6

47: 33, 36, 39, 45, 35

48: 2, 3, −2, 10, 6

49: 55, 49, 53, 44, 46

50: A, B, C, D, E

EXAMPLE
- S
- B
- P
- T
- W

51: N, D, R, L, S

52: H, Y, S, K, L

53: E, D, K, A, F

54: Y, I, S, A, O

55: N, T, B, P, L

56: D, P, S, T, C

EXAMPLE
- ST
- US
- UT
- UV
- SW

57: JV, VJ, HE, HC, FG

58: TV, ZU, XY, UZ, VW

59: NC, CD, VU, UV, ZA

60: LA, CZ, LC, ZC, ZB

61: TP, PQ, RS, GT, PT

62: TU, LZ, ZL, VW, XM

EXAMPLE
- hard
- rough
- challenging
- strict
- solid

63: roll, spin, wind, cake, swivel

64: regard, discolour, clean, spot, liquid

65: huge, mountain, up, graph, scale

66: sympathetic, tender, hard-hearted, brisk, sickly

67: rope, fling, band, sling, chuck

68: overpriced, valued, buy, agreement, dear

EXAMPLE
- loop
- real
- peal
- role
- leap

69: pet, sit, fit, rid, let

70: fib, far, sat, fat, rat

71: stem, mate, meat, mope, post

72: pill, skin, pins, pink, silk

73: rank, milk, silk, kiln, mask

74: trap, plod, part, prod, port

EXAMPLE
- duck
- goat
- cow
- swan
- robin

75: cooperate, undertake, collaborate, continue, unite

76: Africa, France, Antarctica, Asia, Italy

77: tornado, rain, hurricane, sleet, snow

78: wool, silk, cotton, nylon, plastic

79: goldfish, toad, crow, frog, newt

80: arid, moist, parched, wet, thirsty

VERBAL REASONING TEST B

VR B

Pupil's Name: _____
School Name: _____
Date of Test: _____

PUPIL NUMBER, **SCHOOL NUMBER**, **DATE OF BIRTH** (Day, Month, Year) — bubble grid.

Please mark like this ⊢.

EXAMPLE
- table / chair
- cup ☒ / fork
- knife / mug

1. crime / prison / thief / jail / police / offence

2. skip / stagger / stumble / stroll / hop / amble

3. delicate / sturdy / hoarse / pretty / special / fragile

4. swindle / prevent / succumb / ignore / abandon / surrender

5. review / feature / resignation / essay / aspect / assertion

6. blatant / blank / bitter / obvious / corrupt / inconspicuous

EXAMPLE
- Richard ate
- ate his
- his delicious
- delicious breakfast
- breakfast hungrily

7. Paola likes / likes caring / caring for / her little / little brother

8. Mimi bought / bought more / more than / than one / one book

9. Theo read / read to / to the / the young / young boy

10. My school / school had / had the / the best / best uniform

11. The cake / cake is / is just / just about / about ready

12. Petra sang / the final / final song / of the / the show

EXAMPLE
s / t / a / n / d

13. b / l / a / n / k

14. t / h / e / r / e

15. b / a / t / c / h

16. t / a / i / n / t

17. j / e / s / t

18. t / e / a / c / h

EXAMPLE
8 / 7 / 5 / 6 / 4

19. 9 / 11 / 8 / 6 / 4

20. 27 / 26 / 23 / 19 / 22

21. 9 / 10 / 7 / 6 / 8

22. 19 / 39 / 41 / 38 / 32

23. 26 / 22 / 28 / 32 / 23

24. 21 / 20 / 16 / 17 / 18

EXAMPLE
duck / goat / cow / swan / robin

25. book / newspaper / write / sign / magazine

26. light / table / switch / chair / desk

27. high jump / cricket / rugby / hurdles / football

28. square / circle / cube / triangle / sphere

29. chase / recover / pursue / follow / find

30. smell / eye / taste / see / ear

© HarperCollins Publishers Ltd

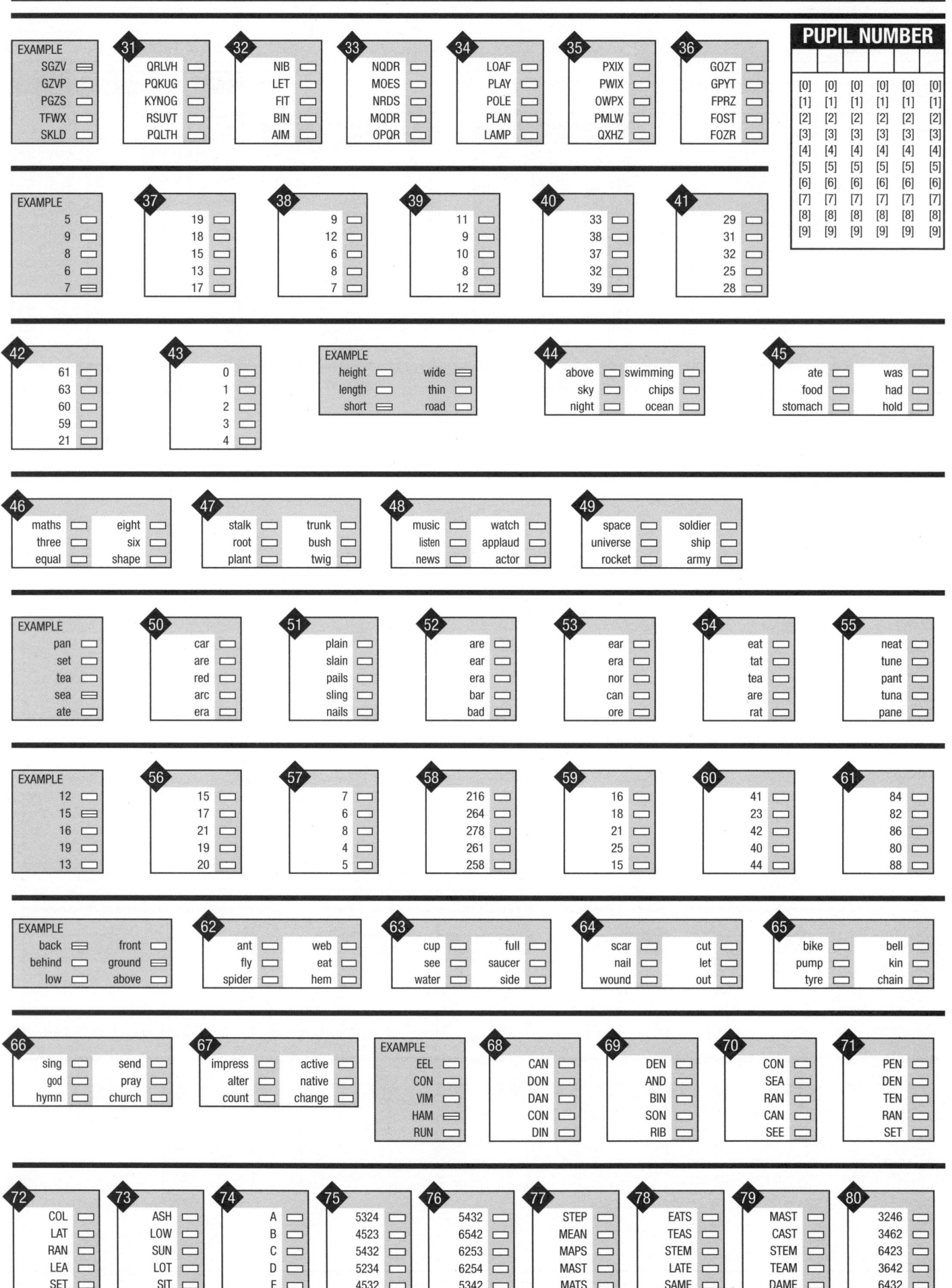

VERBAL REASONING TEST C

VR C

Pupil's Name

School Name

Date of Test

DATE OF BIRTH

Please mark like this ⊢.

EXAMPLE
- duck
- goat ☒
- cow ☒
- swan
- robin

1
- cylinder
- rectangle
- cone
- cuboid
- hexagon

2
- furious
- angry
- upset
- cross
- hurt

3
- tractor
- truck
- ferry
- lorry
- barge

4
- boil
- toast
- oven
- roast
- pan

5
- elude
- run
- avoid
- jog
- dodge

6
- pronoun
- apostrophe
- comma
- adverb
- colon

EXAMPLE
- s
- t ☒
- a
- n
- d

7
- b
- r
- e
- a
- t
- h
- e

8
- s
- i
- g
- h
- t

9
- s
- a
- v
- i
- o
- u
- r

10
- s
- w
- o
- o
- n

11
- f
- e
- v
- e
- r

12
- s
- u
- a
- v
- e

EXAMPLE
- back ☒ front
- behind — ground ☒
- low — above

13
- fed — top
- bud — get
- lid — up

14
- pave — side
- road — meant
- cross — sing

15
- carp — page
- year — post
- ramp — age

16
- suit — ping
- flaw — able
- camp — sight

17
- tie — knot
- but — ton
- eat — up

18
- stock — out
- catch — king
- count — pile

EXAMPLE
- height — wide
- length — thin
- short ☒ road

19
- planned — calculated
- informal — definite
- fancy — suspicious

20
- learn — enemy
- school — private
- student — leader

21
- prudent — exhausting
- clever — exceptional
- sensitive — excessive

22
- hedge — table
- green — cook
- mow — fridge

23
- belt — needle
- strap — cuff
- hit — tie

24
- circle — quadrilateral
- triangle — sphere
- square — symmetry

EXAMPLE
- A
- B
- C
- D
- E

25
- A
- B
- C
- D
- E

26
- A
- B
- C
- D
- E

27
- A
- B
- C
- D
- E

28
- A
- B
- C
- D
- E

29
- A
- B
- C
- D
- E

30
- A
- B
- C
- D
- E

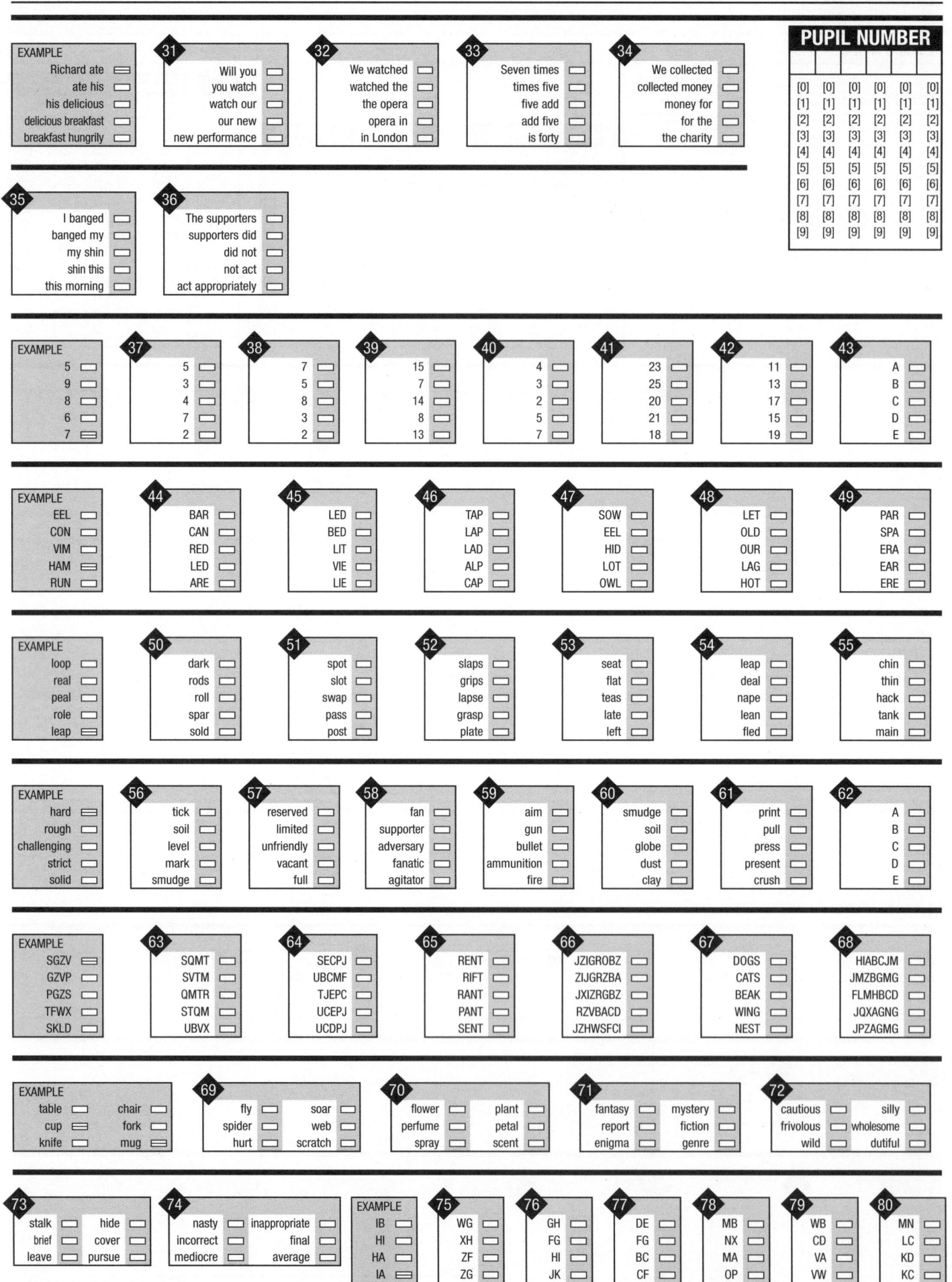

VERBAL REASONING TEST D

VR D

Pupil's Name
School Name
Date of Test
DATE OF BIRTH

Please mark like this ⊢.

EXAMPLE
- pan
- set
- tea
- sea
- ate

1
- bar
- bad
- dab
- oar
- rod

2
- pan
- nap
- asp
- ask
- sap

3
- leg
- log
- lob
- bog
- beg

4
- sea
- see
- raw
- war
- awe

5
- car
- are
- era
- arc
- ear

6
- ore
- con
- nor
- err
- nor

EXAMPLE
- table — chair
- cup — fork
- knife — mug

7
- correct — authentic
- phoney — technical
- peeved — fake

8
- chaos — mayhem
- hectic — suppression
- fury — prudence

9
- faint — gaunt
- wholesome — hefty
- haggard — distinctive

10
- spur — whip
- crave — motivate
- captivate — gallop

11
- push — pull
- flog — thrash
- snare — break

12
- resilient — haughty
- different — vulnerable
- cautious — tough

EXAMPLE
- A
- B
- C
- D
- E

13
- A
- B
- C
- D
- E

14
- A
- B
- C
- D
- E

15
- A
- B
- C
- D
- E

16
- A
- B
- C
- D
- E

17
- A
- B
- C
- D
- E

18
- A
- B
- C
- D
- E

EXAMPLE
- back — front
- behind — ground
- low — above

19
- leg — age
- foot — old
- arm — ankle

20
- hedge — bush
- border — earth
- garden — row

21
- computer — bored
- screen — shot
- key — door

22
- thread — stitch
- sew — pin
- needle — bare

23
- little — some
- trouble — full
- plenty — lot

24
- hood — scarf
- tab — trick
- tape — let

EXAMPLE
- s
- t
- a
- n
- d

25
- s
- h
- a
- r
- e

26
- c
- h
- a
- i
- n

27
- c
- l
- o
- u
- t

28
- c
- o
- a
- s
- t

29
- w
- e
- a
- r
- y

30
- p
- a
- i
- n

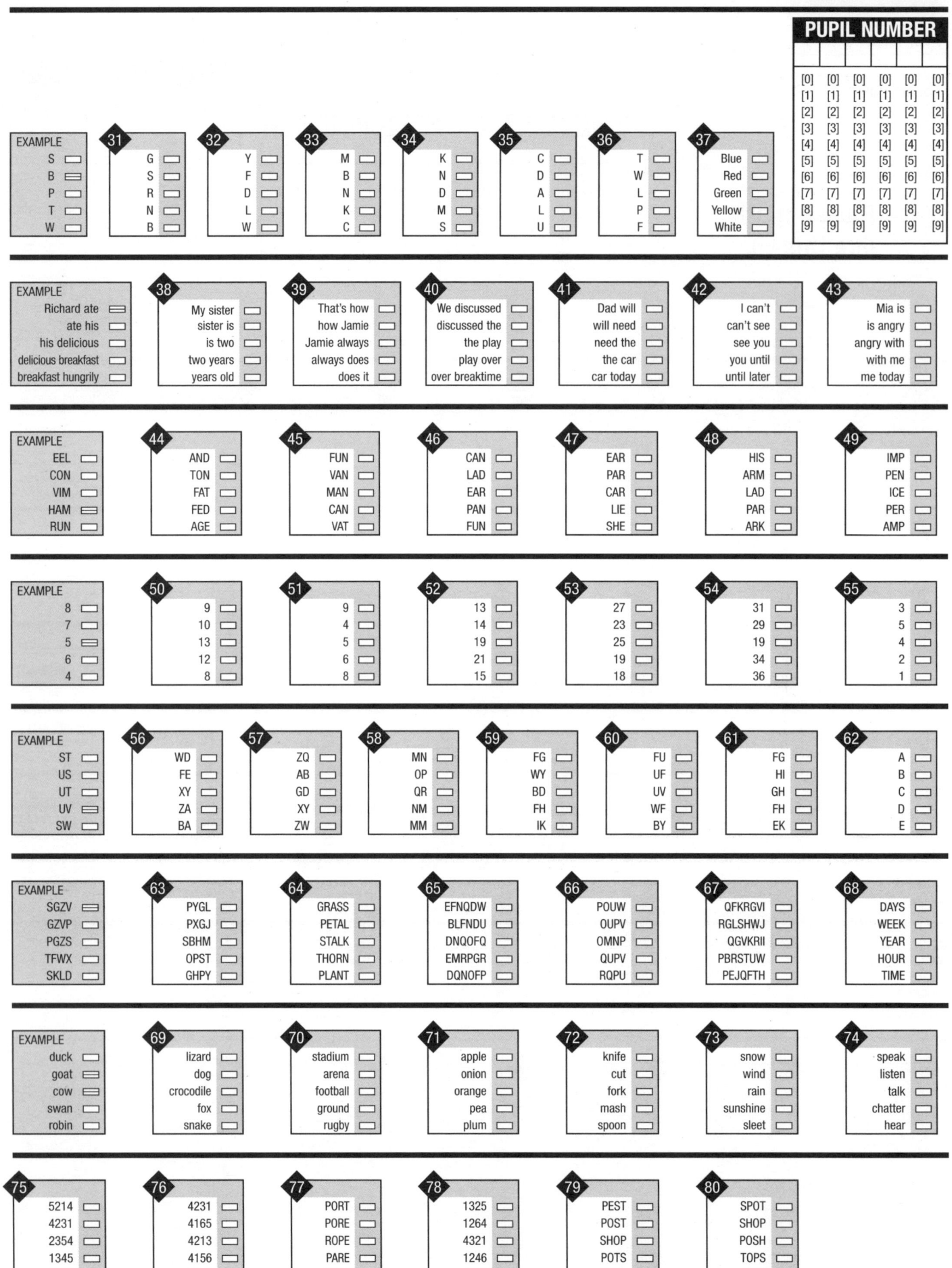